WHO IS THE

Bride?

REBECCA PARK TOTILO

Who Is The Bride?

Copyedited by Rachel A. Park.

Cover Design by Rebecca Park Totilo.

Printed in the United States of America.

Published by Rebecca at the Well Foundation, PO Box
60044, St. Petersburg, Florida 33784.

Scripture references are taken from the King James
Version of the Bible.

ISBN 978-0-9749115-7-1

Table of Contents

> For thy Maker *is* thine husband; the LORD of
> hosts *is* his name; and thy Redeemer the Holy
> One of Israel; The God of the whole earth shall
> he be called.
>
> —Isaiah 54:5

From Genesis to Revelation, the Scriptures reveal Yahweh's desire to have an intimate relationship with mankind and dwell in his presence. Yet, as much as the Creator wanted to lavish His love upon man, He would only do so if man mutually agreed to this relationship. For this reason God created man with a free will, allowing him to choose if he wanted to dwell and walk with God in all eternity. Today, our Heavenly Father continues to extend that choice to His family of believers—allowing them to determine what kind of relationship they want with God.

For each of the different types of relationships described in the Bible—whether it be a body, family, a vineyard or an army—God's greatest desire was for a more intimate relationship—one which could only be pictured between a husband and wife. To demonstrate this, Yahweh chose to use the marriage relationship as a "type or shadow" to the degree of intimacy He wanted with His church.

The marriage between Adam and Eve in the Garden of Eden was a prophetic foreshadow of Yeshua's desire to be married to His bride, the church.

Genesis 2:23-24 says:

And Adam said, This *is* now bone of my bones, and flesh of my flesh: she shall be called Woman, because she was taken out of Man. Therefore shall a man leave his father and his mother, and shall cleave unto his wife: and they shall be one flesh.

These same words are spoken again in the book of Ephesians 5:30-32:

For we are members of his body, of his flesh, and of his bones. For this cause shall a man leave his father and mother, and shall be joined unto his wife, and they two shall be one flesh. This is a great mystery: but I speak concerning Christ and the church.

The Bible gives us parallels between Adam and Yeshua, naming Adam as "the first man Adam" and Yeshua as "the last Adam."

We read in Genesis 1:26, "And God said, Let us make man in our image, after our likeness." In Philippians 2:6-7, we see Yeshua described as being in the likeness of man: "Who, being in the form of God, thought it not robbery to be equal with God: but made himself of no reputation, and took upon him the form of a servant, and was made in the likeness of men." This is mentioned again in 1 Corinthians 15:45-47.

We also see how Adam was named as King of the Earth. Psalm 8:3-6 says:

> When I consider thy heavens, the work of thy fingers, the moon and the stars, which thou hast ordained; what is man, that thou art mindful of him? and the son of man, that thou visitest him? For thou hast made him a little lower than the angels, and hast crowned him with glory and honor. Thou madest him to have dominion over the works of thy hands; thou hast put all *things* under his feet.

All believers know Yeshua is the "King of Kings" as described in Daniel's night vision in 7:13-14:

> I saw in the night visions, and, behold, *one* like the Son of man came with the clouds of heaven, and came to the Ancient of days, and they brought him near before him. And there was given him dominion, and glory, and a king-

dom, that all people, nations, and languages, should serve him: his dominion *is* an everlasting dominion, which shall not pass away, and his kingdom *that* which shall not be destroyed

God created Adam to have dominion over all the earth, ruling and reigning over God's creation as a king over the earth. With his authority, Adam named everything as we can see in Genesis 2:19-20. This is a prophetic picture of Yeshua who has been given the name that is above every name, demonstrating His authority as mentioned in Philippians 2:7-11.

However, God determined it was not good for Adam to be alone, so He formed a help meet for him (Genesis 2:18). The bride was a suitable match for him, completing him. Just as God presented a "suitable" mate for Adam, so He will present Yeshua, the last Adam, with a suitable bride.

The Scriptures tell us that God caused a deep sleep to fall upon Adam. Genesis 2:21 says, "And the LORD God caused a deep sleep to fall upon Adam, and he slept: and he took one of his ribs, and closed up the flesh instead thereof."

This picture of "deep sleep" is also a prophetic shadow, as mentioned by Yeshua in John 11:11-14:

These things said he: and after that he saith unto them, Our friend Lazarus sleepeth; but I go, that I may awake him out of sleep. Then said his disciples, Lord, if he sleep, he shall do well. Howbeit Jesus spake of his death: but they thought that he had spoken of taking of rest in sleep. Then said Jesus unto them plainly, Lazarus is dead.

Sleep, a synonymous term for death in the Bible, is a spiritual picture of death of the flesh followed by resurrection concerning the Lord. We can read about this in 1 Thessalonians 4:14-17 and 1 Corinthians 15:51-53.

Adam's side being pierced or wounded was a spiritual picture of Yeshua's crucifixion on the cross. Isaiah 53:5 tells us, "But he *was* wounded for our transgressions, *he was* bruised for our iniquities: the chastisement of our peace *was* upon him."

Following this incision to remove one of Adam's rib (a small remnant), God fashions Eve; thus, the wedding in the Garden of Eden is a prophetic picture of His bride, the church, who will come out from the body of Messiah, through the shedding of blood.

Just as Eve was taken from the side of Adam (his rib was taken from his body), so the Bride of Christ will be taken from Yeshua's body. Yeshua's bride will be taken out from His body of believers from among those who are saved.

The bride in Scriptures is pictured as a female, though the distinction of His bride being made up of males and females is irrelevant. There is no gender in our heavenly position in Messiah. Scriptures tell us we are all sons of God through faith. Galatians 3:28 says, "There is neither Jew nor Greek, there is neither bond nor free, there is neither male nor female: for you are all one in Christ Jesus."

Many Christians today believe the "body" and "Bride of Christ" are synonymous terms. However, that is simply not true. The Greek word, *Ekklesia*, means "congregation of believers" as referred to as His body in Ephesians 1:22-23. The definition of "church" is "called out ones" and refers to the remnant that came out from the body and is set apart for Him alone.

Not everyone who has received the gift of salvation will respond to this closer walk. Believers who continue to live a worldly, or carnal, lifestyle will not be ready to meet the Bridegroom.

And he cried mightily with a strong voice, saying, Babylon the great is fallen, is fallen, and is become the habitation of devils, and the hold of every foul spirit, and a cage of every unclean and hateful bird. And I heard another voice from heaven, saying, Come out of her, my people, that ye be not partakers of her sins, and that ye receive not of her plagues.

—Revelation 18:2

In Genesis, the story of Abraham seeking a bride for his son, Isaac, is clearly a prophetic picture of how God, the Father, desires a bride for His son, Yeshua. Abraham represents God the Father, who sends His servant, Eliezer, representing the Holy Spirit (*Ruach HaKodesh*), to His family, representing Israel (and those grafted in) for His son, Isaac, a type of Christ. Rebekah is a spiritual picture of the Bride of Christ.

Abraham instructed his servant to not go to the Canaanites, a picture of the world (and those of the world), but to seek a bride for his son from among his family or own people. This clearly demonstrates this was not a calling out for "salvation" among the heathen. Abraham instructions were clear to his servant to take a wife for Isaac from among his kindred (family or body).

We are reminded in Galatians 3:16, 29:

> Now to Abraham and his seed were the promises made. He saith not, And to seeds, as of many; but as of one, And to thy seed, which is Christ. And if ye *be* Christ's, then are ye Abraham's seed, and heirs according to the promise.

Spiritually, all true believers in the Messiah are the spiritual seed of Abraham and members of his family. In Romans 4:16 it tells us Abraham is the father of our faith.

Abraham makes his servant swear an oath to not take a wife from among the Canaanites, who represent spiritual idolatry. This is true for Yeshua's bride as well.

When God gave the *Torah* to the children of Jacob at Mount Sinai, He instructed them to completely destroy the Canaanite culture, to not serve there gods, and to not make marriages with them. God warned that His judgment would come upon them if they did. Deuteronomy 7:1-4 says:

> When the LORD thy God shall bring thee into the land whither thou goest to possess it, and hath cast out many nations before thee, the

Hittites, and the Girgashites, and the Amorites, and the Canaanites, and the Perizzites, and the Hivites, and the Jebusites, seven nations greater and mightier than thou; and when the LORD thy God shall deliver them before thee; thou shalt smite them, *and* utterly destroy them; thou shalt make no covenant with them, nor show mercy unto them; neither shalt thou make marriages with them; thy daughter thou shalt not give unto his son, nor his daughter shalt thou take unto thy son. For they will turn away thy son from following me, that they may serve other gods: so will the anger of the LORD be kindled against you, and destroy thee suddenly.

In the same way, God will not marry a bride who lives according to the world and follows after other gods.

Abraham told his servant where he could find his son a bride in Genesis 24:10:

And the servant took ten camels of the camels of his master, and departed; for all the goods of his master *were* in his hand: and he arose, and went to Mesopotamia, unto the city of Nahor.

Genesis 11:27 tells us Nahor was the brother of Abraham. The city of Nahor in Mesopotamia was located in

Babylon. Spiritually, this is a prophetic picture that the Bride of Christ will be taken from Babylon.

Babylon is a picture of the world, and spiritual idolatry. This Bible story shows us God's bride coming out of Babylon, and the Holy Spirit is calling her to follow Him to the spiritual promised land, Zion.

The Bride is a Family Member

And Abraham said unto his eldest servant of his house, that ruled over all that he had, Put, I pray thee, thy hand under my thigh: and I will make thee swear by the LORD, the God of heaven, and the God of the earth, that thou shalt not take a wife unto my son of the daughters of the Canaanites, among whom I dwell: but thou shalt go unto my country, and to my kindred, and take a wife unto my son Isaac.

—Genesis 24:2-4

In the beginning, God acted as the first *Shadkhan*, or matchmaker, commanding Adam and Eve to cleave together as "one flesh." Eve, taken from Adam's body, became the first bride.

We read in Genesis 24 how Abraham's servant Eliezer, which means "God's helper" in Hebrew, acted as a matchmaker modeled after the Heavenly Father and found the suitable bride for Abraham's son, Isaac. Abraham, having realized the Canaanite women whom he lived among were morally unsuitable, sent Eliezer to find the perfect match from among his own family and of his father's house.

In the same way, God the Father sent His helper, the Holy Spirit, to His kindred, from among God's people to take a bride for His son, Yeshua. He invites all who are members of His family to become the bride.

In Genesis 24:4, Abraham instructs his servant to "go unto my country, and to my kindred." He also told his servant to not take his son Isaac back again (verse 6). This depicts how the Holy Spirit is to seek a bride while Christ is to remain in Heaven with the Father, until the time comes for God to restore all things (Acts 3:20-21). Just as Abraham's servant Eliezer had charge over all he had (Genesis 24:2), so the Holy Spirit has all of the Heavenly Father's resources at His disposal.

Notice that it is the Bridegroom (or bridegroom's father/servant) who selected the bride (not vice-versa). Yahweh/Yeshua is always the one who initiates the love relationship with His bride. He chose and selected us, as Scripture says in 1 John 4:19, "We love him, because he first loved us." And, in John 15:16: "Ye have not chosen me, but I have chosen you, and ordained you, that ye should go and bring forth fruit, and *that* your fruit should remain."

The Bride is One

Behold, thou *art* fair, my love; behold, thou *art*
fair; thou *hast* doves' eyes within thy locks.
—Song of Solomon 4:1a

God designed the bond of "oneness" in order for us
to grow and deepen our relationship with Yeshua and have
eyes only for Him.

One who has "doves' eyes" is seen as beautiful, like a
turtledove with singleness of purpose and devotion to her
mate for a lifetime. As believers, our eyes should be of
spiritual perception, veiled with a beauty and love set apart
for the Messiah alone.

The dove, a bird of love and sorrow, also served as
an offering and sacrifice upon the altar for poor families,
such as in the case of Mary and Joseph's two turtledoves
offering in Luke 2:23-24. It is also symbolic of the *Ruach
HaKodesh*, as seen in Matthew 3:16, when the Holy Spirit
came upon the Lord as a dove and helped the Messiah
complete His ministry while here on the earth.

The Lord desires to see the reflection of His *Ruach HaKodesh* (Holy Spirit) in our eyes. It is the Spirit that gently woos believers to come into a deeper intimacy and helps us prepare as the bride, just as Hegai, the king's servant, helped Esther prepare for her king.

In the Song of Solomon 6:7-10 it says,

> As a piece of a pomegranate *are* thy temples within thy locks. There are threescore queens, and fourscore concubines, and virgins without number. My dove, my undefiled is *but* one; she *is* the *only* one of her mother, she *is* the choice *one* of her that bore her. The daughters saw her, and blessed her; *yea*, the queens and the concubines, and they praised her. Who *is* she *that* looketh forth as the morning, fair as the moon, clear as the sun, *and* terrible as *an army* with banners?

Many followers have entered in through the door of salvation and are part of the Body of Christ and will enter into Heaven. But their hearts have turned away from the Holy Spirit's invitation to enter into a deeper intimacy with the Messiah. The Lord calls those followers His concubines, queens, and virgins, as seen in Song of Solomon 6:8. The Bible says in Matthew 22:14, "For many are called, but few *are* chosen." In this Scripture "are" is italicized—it was added by the editors and should read, "few choose." It is we who will determine how close we want to be with out Savior.

Revelation 3:20 says, "Behold, I stand at the door, and knock: if any man hear my voice, and open the door, I will come in to him, and will sup with him, and he with me."

Our Heavenly Bridegroom refers to His beloved bride as the only "one" who has said yes to His request— "Open to me"—and has entered into a deeper relationship, identifying with the shame of His sufferings and the full mystery of His death on the cross.

The Bride is Set Apart

But as he which hath called you is holy, so be ye
holy in all manner of conversation; because it is
written, Be ye holy; for I am holy.

—1 Peter 1:15-16

The Hebrew word for marriage is *Kiddushin*, which
means "sanctification or holiness." It comes from the root
word *Kodesh* which means "holy, to be set apart," and *Kadash*,
which means "sanctified and separated from evil." God has
elevated marriage to a holy state by introducing Himself to
the relationship—thus we have "Holy Matrimony." Just as
God is holy, we are to be holy as it says in Leviticus 11:44:
"For I *am* the LORD your God: ye shall therefore sanctify
yourselves, and ye shall be holy; for I *am* holy."

Most Christians think of holy as sinless, but biblically
it means that you have grown in spiritually maturity and have
an intimate relationship with the Savior—set apart for His
service. We are reminded in 1 Peter 1:15-16 that what we
say is directly related to our holiness as well.

In biblical times, an Israeli bridegroom proposed to
his beloved by offering the *Kiddush* cup, which means "cup

of sanctification or holiness." If his chosen accepted his marriage proposal, she sipped from the cup and was now betrothed and promised in marriage to him.

Yeshua kept the same wedding custom after the Passover meal, offering the *Kiddush* cup to His disciples. Now, when believers take Holy Communion, they are entering into or renewing their wedding vow to Yeshua, our Bridegroom. However, as we see in Revelation 18, Satan entices all to drink from His cup of wine of wrath and commit fornication with him. The church is entirely espoused to Yeshua, but not all members will make it to the altar. The bride must remain faithful to Him by not partaking in the ways of the world, remaining separate.

Revelation 18:3 says:

> For all nations have drunk of the wine of the wrath of her fornication, and the kings of the earth have committed fornication with her and the merchants of the earth are waxed rich through the abundance of her delicacies.

In the ancient times, the Jewish betrothal occurred one or two years before the actual wedding (or nuptials) and involved making a covenant. The Hebrew word for "covenant" is *B'rit*, and this was actually quite more serious than an engagement today. In biblical times, a covenant was final, sealed in blood, and legally binding, as we see in the relationship between Mary and Joseph. Matthew 1:18-19 says:

22

Now the birth of Jesus Christ was on this wise: When as his mother Mary was espoused to Joseph, before they came together, she was found with child of the Holy Ghost. Then Joseph her husband, being a just *man,* and not willing to make her a public example, was minded to put her away privily.

While Mary and Joseph were espoused (betrothed), he thought to put her away (divorce her) since he believed she had been unfaithful. Their covenant was so binding that it would require a bill of divorce to break.

This same word "espoused" in Matthew 1:18-19 is used by Paul as he reminds the believers at the Corinthian church to remain faithful. It says in 2 Corinthians 11:2: "For I am jealous over you with godly jealousy: for I have espoused you to one husband, that I may present *you as* a chase virgin to Christ."

The entire body is espoused to the Messiah; however, not all will be at the wedding. Many believers today are unfaithful and there is a possibly the Lord will "put them away." This does not mean the loss of their salvation, but a loss of rewards when Yeshua returns, as seen in 1 John 2:28, Titus 3:8 and 2 John 1:8.

To be a part of the Bride of Christ is a great reward to those Christians who have lived a pure and holy life for the Messiah. Some may not remain fully devoted to Him and will set their affections on other things above Yeshua, thus committing spiritual adultery. 2 Corinthians 11:3 says, "But I fear, lest by any means, as the serpent beguiled Eve through his subtlety, so your minds should be corrupted from the simplicity that is in Christ." Yeshua desires His people to be watchful and pray. Luke 21:36 tells us, "Watch ye therefore, and pray always, that ye may be accounted worthy to escape all these things that shall come to pass, and to stand before the Son of man."

The Bride has a Marriage Contract

Behold, the days come, saith the LORD, that I
will make a new covenant with the house of Israel, and with the house of Judah: not according
to the covenant that I made with their fathers in
the day *that* I took them by the hand to bring
them out of the land of Egypt; which my covenant they broke, although I was a husband unto
them, saith the LORD: but this *shall be* the
covenant that I will make with the house of Israel; After those days, saith the LORD, I will
put my law in their inward parts, and write it in
their hearts; and will be their God, and they
shall be my people.

—Jeremiah 31:31-33

In a traditional betrothal, the engaged couple enters
into a covenant with the signing of the *Ketubah*, or marriage
contract. In this marriage contract are the terms of their
agreement, such as the bride price and provisions the
bridegroom agrees to make. It also names the wife as the
heir to the estate, should he die.

It is for this reason that they have a wedding ceremony—to sanctify and bless the contract. Properly signed and witnessed, the document is given to the bride, and she is instructed to keep it with her at all times, since there can be no marital relations if it is lost or destroyed.

Rich in commitment, the *Ketubah* is read aloud for all to hear of their mutual devotion toward one another. The custom of reading the *Ketubah* aloud is rooted in the great wedding between God and Israel, when Moses received the Torah.

While Moses was on the mountain-top with God receiving the Ten Commandments, the bride was committing spiritual adultery with the golden calf. Upon returning, Moses' anger kindled within him and he broke the tablets of stone (acting on behalf of the bride), which was symbolic of breaking the marriage contract.

God warned Israel at Mount Sinai after He spoke the ten words to them, that if they didn't enter into the cloud (symbolic of the *Huppah* or wedding canopy), they would fall into the temptation of idolatry. Yet, God's people insisted God talk to Moses.

If believers today refuse to enter into the deeper things of God with Him (symbolic of the cloud at Mount Sinai), they will place themselves in a position of falling into temptation, just as the Israelites did.

After Moses destroyed the golden calf (putting to death the adulterous lover), as *Torah* commands, 3,000 others were put to death—the perpetrators of this evil. Interestingly, this is the same number of souls converted at *Shavuot*, or Pentecost.

When God's people mourned and repented, Moses interceded for the people and found grace in God's sight. The Scriptures tells us in Exodus 34:6-7:

> And the Lord passed by before him, and proclaimed, The LORD, The LORD God, merciful and gracious, longsuffering, and abundant in goodness and truth, keeping mercy for thousands, forgiving iniquity and transgression and sin.

Yeshua's beloved bride honors her marriage contract by upholding the entire Word of God, not committing spiritual adultery. She allows the Lord to write it upon her heart.

In the mouth of two or three witnesses shall
every word be established.

—2 Corinthians 13:1

Like any legal transaction, the marriage contract required two witnesses present for the presentation to the
bride. These two witnesses represented Moses and Elijah.
Moses is known as the attendant to the bride, while Elijah is
the attendant to the bridegroom. We see these two attendants with Yeshua on the Mount of Transfiguration, a
prophetic picture of what He shall be like at the marriage
supper. Matthew 17:1-3 tells us:

> And after six days Jesus taketh Peter, James,
> and John his brother, and bringeth them up
> into an high mountain apart, and was transfig-
> ured before them: and his face did shine as the
> sun, and his raiment was white as the light.
> And, behold, there appeared unto them Moses
> and Elijah talking with him.

We also read in Revelation 11:3, "And I will give
power unto my two witnesses, and they shall prophesy a

thousand two hundred *and* threescore days, clothed in sackcloth."

The remnant that makes up the bride is a company of two witnesses. This concept of two witnesses is clear in the story of Jacob, who is now called Israel by God. He spent a restless night wrestling with an angel upon meeting his brother, Esau—whom he had cheated out of his birthright. Thus, he named the place *Mahanaim*, which means "two camps."

When Jacob received word of Esau's arrival with 400 men, he greatly feared, dividing his two wives, Leah and Rachel and their children, into two camps.

Prophetically, God also divided Israel into the house of Judah, the southern kingdom, and the house of Israel/Ephraim, the northern kingdom. Both houses went into captivity—Ephraim to Assyria, and 125 years later, Judah to Babylon. Only Judah returned to the land, along with some of Ephraim, while the rest dispersed into the culture of the Assyrians and scattered across the face of the earth into all the nations.

Just as two witnesses are required as eyewitnesses to the signing of the marriage contract or *Ketubah*, Ephraim and Judah (a picture of Jews and Gentiles) make up Israel, the one true Bride of Messiah. Both serve as witnesses and give testimony to what God has done in the past, and is doing now to bring about His kingdom on this earth. It is those that make up these two camps that will be the two witnesses in the earth during the latter days.

All true believers in the Messiah are a part of Israel, whether naturally or grafted in. Romans 11:17 says, "And if some of the branches be broken off, and thou, being a wild olive tree, wert grafted in among them, and with them partakest of the root and fatness of the olive tree."

God has not replaced His bride Israel with the "New Testament" believers, as some teach in the body today. The Bride of Christ is made up of all believers in Messiah, whether Jew or Gentile, and make up the commonwealth of Israel. 1 Corinthians 12:13 reads, "For by one Spirit are we all baptized into one body, whether *we be* Jews or Gentiles, whether *we be* bond or free; and have been all made to drink into one Spirit."

Yeshua says He is the same yesterday, today and for-ever. Therefore, God hasn't changed brides and He certainly doesn't have two. Some teach that God is married to Israel and Yeshua to the church. But Yeshua said that the Father and He were one—and He is the one true God. So that doctrine would make God a polygamist.

The book of Hosea is a great picture of God's pur-suant love and even after Israel (Ephraim and Judah) committed spiritual adultery and iniquity against Him. Hosea 2:19-20 says:

And I will betroth thee unto me forever; yea, I will betroth thee unto me in righteousness, and in judgment, and in lovingkindness, and in mercies. I will even betroth thee unto me in faithfulness: and thou shalt know the LORD.

God commanded Hosea to take an adulterous woman as his wife and to continue to seek her and bring her back, as a picture of how Israel had committed great whoredom against Him, departing from the Lord—yet, He promised to bring back to Himself. Hosea 3:1-5 tells us:

Then said the LORD unto me, Go yet, love a woman beloved of *her* friend, yet an adulteress, according to the love of the LORD toward the children of Israel, who look to other gods, and love flagons of wine. So I bought her to me for fifteen *pieces* of silver, and *for* a homer of barley, and a half homer of barley: and I said unto her, Thou shalt abide for me many days; thou shalt not play the harlot, and thou shalt not be for *another* man: so *will* I also *be* for thee. For the children of Israel shall abide many days without a king, and without a prince, and without a sacrifice, and without an image, and without an ephod, and *without* teraphim; afterward shall the children of Israel return, and seek the LORD their God, and David their king; and shall fear the LORD and his goodness in the latter days.

Many in the church today are like Ephraim, having turned away from their Hebraic roots and chasing after the pagan ways of the world. Even Judah has become defiled. Though they have guarded God's law, they have been blind to the advancing light and the revelation of Yeshua the Messiah in these last days.

Just as the two thieves on the crosses beside Yeshua stood as witnesses to His obligation in His blood covenant, so we His bride will stand as a testimony to what Yahweh is doing in the last days, as Gentiles and Israel—both make up the Bride of Christ.

And said, Whose daughter *art* thou? Tell me, I
pray thee: is there room *in* thy father's house for
us to lodge in?

—Genesis 24:23

In Genesis 24, when Eliezer found Abraham's family, he asked Rebekah if there was room in her father's house
for lodging.

The Hebrew word for "lodge" is *Loon*, which means
"to stay permanently, to abide all night." The word "room"
in Hebrew is *Makom*, a term for heaven and God's throne.

Here we have another spiritual picture of Yeshua de-
siring to marry His bride in His father's house—and when
the marriage is consummated she will abide permanently in
His presence forever. There are two references to this, one
found in Jeremiah 17:12 and another in Genesis 28:17. In
Genesis 28:17, we read: "And he was afraid, and said, How
dreadful *is* this place! this *is* none other but the house of
God, and this *is* the gate of heaven."

This is where Jacob had a dream and saw a ladder reaching the top of heaven. The term "place" is mentioned three times in Genesis 28:11. God is highlighting something significant about this word and what is happening.

In Genesis 28:11, it says, "And he lighted upon a certain place, and tarried there all night, because the sun was set; and he took of the stones of that place, and put *them for* his pillows, and lay down in that place to sleep."

The Hebrew word for "sleep" in Genesis 28:11 is *Shakav*, which means "to lie down, for rest, sexual connection." The Hebrew word for "sleep" in Genesis 28:16 is *Shaynah*, which means "to sleep."

In Genesis 28:16, Jacob awoke from his sleep. And, this time the word "sleep" is not the same word in Hebrew as in verse 11. God is communicating something spiritual through Jacob's dream, and the sleep he was experiencing was a prophetic picture of something for the future. Could it be a prophetic picture of a marriage happening at a place called *Makom*, the House of God? Jacob awoke in awe because of his awareness of this place where he slept.

Isaiah 26:2 speaks of the gates of heaven: "Open ye the gates, that the righteous nation which keepeth the truth may enter in."

And Psalm 118:19-20 says, "Open to me the gates of righteousness: I will go into them, *and* I will praise the

LORD: This gate of the LORD, into which the righteous shall enter."

Here we see a prophetic picture of the bride being taken to the House of God to participate in the wedding between Yeshua and His bride. It also demonstrates that His bride must keep the truth of God which is His Word. We read on to see that Jacob in Genesis 28:19 called the place *Bethel*, which means in Hebrew, "House of God."

A special place that the groom is away preparing awaits the bride, while she must also be busy preparing for her big day. We read in Revelation 19:7, "Let us be glad and rejoice, and give honor to him: for the marriage of the Lamb is come, and his wife hath made herself ready."

The bride and bridegroom spend seven days (one week) in the *Huppah*—symbolic of the days of creation.

2 Peter 3:8 says that one day is as one thousand years to the Lord. Presently, we are in the sixth day, and the Millennium reign will begin on the seventh day, which is the Sabbath—the day of rest. His bride will enter His rest for 1,000 years, symbolic of the Sabbath.

Following the seven days in the *huppah* (symbolic of the number of years since creation), the guests will celebrate and wave tabrets in worship with complete abandonment to the Lord.

The Bride has Attendants

> Then shall the kingdom of heaven be likened
> unto ten virgins, which took their lamps, and
> went forth to meet the bridegroom.
>
> —Matthew 25:1

In ancient Israel, it was customary for the bride to
have attendants. These bridesmaids mentioned in the Bible
were called "virgins." As Paul told the Corinthian church,
we are "betrothed to one husband," so that he may present
us as a "pure virgin."

In the parable of the ten virgins, the term "bride" is
not mentioned, but all of the virgins who are "called" and
"invited" to the wedding could qualify to be a bride.

Their duties played a very important part in the marriage procession. Each virgin was given a lamp and instructed to keep it filled with oil so that it would burn
brightly, in order to light the bride's path.

For the Jews, the number "ten" represents a legal
congregation, or *Minyan.* Therefore, the Church, or entire

congregation of true believers in the Messiah, is clearly represented by the ten virgins in the parable Yeshua told.

According to Jewish custom, the virgins stayed close by with the bride, waiting for the groom to come because they didn't know what day or hour he would arrive. All of the virgins robed in white went forth "to meet the bridegroom," leaving their families, homes, and friends temporarily to be a part of the bride's entourage. They anxiously congregated in the same location where they "slumbered and slept" so they could all hear the cry by the groom's attendant in the streets. At the announcement, there was only enough time for the virgins to make their final preparations.

As a member of the bridal party, it is up to each one of us to work out our own salvation and seek God for wisdom and understanding. We can no longer rely on the "teachings of men," but must spend time with our Bridegroom alone, in order to know Him and prepare, for it could be any day or hour.

Matthew 25:13 warns us, "Watch therefore, for ye know neither the day nor the hour wherein the Son of Man cometh."

In Matthew 25:1-13 Yeshua tells us:

Then shall the kingdom of heaven be likened unto ten virgins, which took their lamps, and went forth to meet the bridegroom. And five of them were wise, and five were foolish. They that were foolish took their lamps, and took no oil with them: but the wise took oil in their vessels with their lamps. While the bridegroom tarried, they all slumbered and slept. And at midnight there was a cry made, Behold, the bridegroom cometh; go ye out to meet him. Then all those virgins arose, and trimmed their lamps. And the foolish said unto the wise, Give us of your oil; for our lamps are gone out. But the wise answered, saying, Not so; lest there be not enough for us and you: but go ye rather to them that sell, and buy for yourselves. And while they went to buy, the bridegroom came; and they that were ready went in with him to the marriage: and the door was shut. Afterward came also the other virgins, saying, Lord, Lord, open to us. But he answered and said, Verily I say unto you, I know you not. Watch therefore, for ye know neither the day nor the hour wherein the Son of man cometh.

The Hebrew word *B'toolah* means "to separate, a virgin, a bride, or a city or state."

The ten virgins in this parable represent those Christians who are betrothed to Yeshua (have accepted Him as their Lord and Savior) and will go to heaven. The distinction between the ten virgins, however, was that five were wise and five were foolish based on the presence or absence of oil. This parable is very important to understand, as it speaks of a distinguishing and separation among the body of Christ. While there is a distinction, the kingdom of heaven is likened to ten virgins, not five; therefore, all ten virgins are part of the kingdom. 2 Corinthians 11:2 reminds us that believers are called "virgins," symbolic of being born again.

All of the virgins had lamps, which is symbolic of the Word of God. Psalm 119:105 says, "Thy word *is* a lamp unto my feet, and a light unto my path." The wise virgins proved to be smart for keeping an extra flask of oil, as they were *Torah* observant, or Sabbath-keepers, and wanted to always be prepared, since it would be unlawful for them to buy on the seventh day. They did not know what hour the groom would arrive and wanted to be ready. Although all of the virgins went out to meet the bridegroom and looked forward to His return (this certainly would not be true of the unsaved), the five foolish were not prepared for His delay. Only the wise had an abundant supply of oil, which is symbolic of the *Ruach HaKodesh* (Holy Spirit).

While the foolish virgins went out searching for the merchants to buy more oil, the bridegroom came for those that were ready to enter the marriage with him, and the doors were shut. When the indifferent and careless virgins finally arrived at the banquet hall and said, "open to us," the Lord replied, "I never knew you." The foolish virgins were obviously members of the bridal party—saved and had eternal life. They even heard the "cry" in the streets when the bridegroom arrived, having some understanding of the

Holy Spirit. What they didn't realize was their lack until it was too late.

The foolish virgins do eventually realize their problem and lack of "oil." Instead of having made adequate preparations, they now try to rely upon others. But the wise virgins are unwilling to share their oil, for it is something that needs to be obtained legitimately—and they were not the source of this oil.

The prudent virgins with the extra vessel of oil advised the foolish to go buy it from those who sell it. Instead of seeking the Heavenly Father, the foolish left the light and went into the dark streets, seeking after merchants. They depended on sellers (preachers) for their oil and understanding instead of seeking the truth and knowing the Lord on their own.

The bridegroom does return at the "midnight hour," which is symbolic of the very last moment of the end of days. Some believers, like the foolish virgins, will not be prepared for the delay in His return. The virgins that went in to the marriage were "those that were ready."

Interestingly, the number "five" in Scriptures is symbolic of mortal inadequacy and the need for the grace of God. All believers need God's grace to walk by faith in keeping and honoring God's *Torah*.

The Greek word for "foolish" is *Moros*, which means "dull, sluggish, and stupid." These same foolish virgins are the same ones we see in Luke 13:25 that say they have eaten and drunk in Yeshua's presence, and he calls "workers of iniquity." Luke 13:22-28 shows us:

> And he went through the cities and villages, teaching, and journeying toward Jerusalem. Then said one unto him, Lord, are there few that be saved? And he said unto them, Strive to enter in at the strait gate: for many, I say unto you, will seek to enter in, and shall not be able. When once the master of the house is risen up, and hath shut to the door, and ye begin to stand without, and to knock at the door, saying, Lord, Lord, open unto us; and he shall answer and say unto you, I know you not whence you are: then shall ye begin to say, We have eaten and drunk in thy presence, and thou hast taught in our streets. But he shall say, I tell you, I know you not whence ye are; depart from me, all ye workers of iniquity. There shall be weeping and gnashing of teeth, when ye shall see Abraham, and Isaac, and Jacob, and all the prophets, in the kingdom of God, and you yourselves thrust out.

The foolish virgins have eaten and drank in His presence (attended church) and taught in the streets—but will be wailing and gnashing their teeth and crying, "Lord, Lord, open to us." Yeshua said "few" who go through the straight gate and narrow way are those who consummate the wedding according to Luke 13:25, and are the wise virgins in Matthew 25.

The foolish virgins will be in heaven, but will lose eternal rewards because they chose to walk the "broad" way. They failed to separate themselves from the world and overcome the desires of the flesh—having a spotted wedding garment.

The wise virgins walk the narrow way, dedicating their lives to God and holiness, and separating themselves from the ways of the world and flesh.

In the congregation of believers, some are foolish (carnal Christians) and some are wise (Bride of Christ). Another parallel scripture to Luke 13:22-27 is found in Matthew 7:21-23:

> Not every one that saith unto me, Lord, Lord, shall enter into the kingdom of heaven; but he that doeth the will of my Father which is in heaven. Many will say to me in that day, Lord, Lord, have we not prophesied in thy name? and in thy name have cast out devils? and in thy name done many wonderful works? And then will I profess unto them, I never knew you: depart from me, ye that work iniquity.

This scripture is not against the manifestation of the miracles of the Holy Spirit, but against those who are "workers of iniquity." Therefore, those that are being left out of the bridal chamber are those carnal Christians who are not the bride because they practice iniquity.

The Greek word *Anomia* means "iniquity." It comes from the root word *Anomos*, which is *Nomos*—meaning "law or *Torah*"—plus *A* (negative participle) meaning "without." What Yeshua is referring to is "those without the law."

Those who practice iniquity are those who are called by God and minister with the manifestation of the Holy Spirit but break the *Torah* (God's commandments), teaching others to do so. The body of Christ has been deceived in believing that God's instructions are not for Christians and don't apply to them. Those who teach this will be among those who are "least" in the Kingdom of Heaven. Matthew 5:19 says:

> Whosoever therefore shall break one of these least commandments, and shall teach men so, he shall be called the least in the kingdom of heaven: but whosoever shall do and teach them, the same shall be called great in the kingdom of heaven.

Many have been taught to believe that Paul's explanation in the book of Romans says we are not under the law but under grace, and that the law doesn't apply to New Testament believers. Keeping the law will not save you, but Yeshua said in Matthew 5:17-18:

> Think not that I am come to destroy the law, or the prophets: I am not come to destroy, but to fulfill. For verily I say unto you, Till heaven and earth pass, one jot or one tittle shall in no wise pass from the law, till all be fulfilled.

Mature believers, such as those that make up the bride, understand that just because Yeshua paid the penalty for sin and death on the cross doesn't give believers a license to sin and commit adultery, right? It is the law that teaches us what sin is, so we know what pleases God. Psalm 119:142 says, "Thy righteousness *is* an everlasting righteousness, and thy law *is* the truth."

Matthew 25:11-12 reads, "Afterward came also the other virgins, saying, Lord, Lord, open to us. But he answered and said, Verily I say unto you, I know you not." The Greek word for "know" is *Ginosko*, which means "to understand completely, recognize, what is known is of value or importance, connection of union between man and woman." The Hebrew word for "know" is *Yadah*, which means "to know intimately, sexually." This is the same word used to describe Adam knowing Eve intimately when she conceived.

Interestingly, it is the same word for "wit," as when Eliezer saw Rebekah do exactly as he had prayed and was astonished by God's answer.

Genesis 24:21 shows us, "And the man wondering at her held his peace, to know whether the LORD had made his journey prosperous or not." The "journey," *Derek* in Hebrew, means "the course of life." It had been long and difficult using the transportation of camels, yet he trusted God to provide for his master's son.

God's bride will follow after the heart and will of God, trusting in Him through the trials and tribulations in life to reach the final destination—and in doing so will have intimate knowledge and relationship with Him. It's a lifestyle for the bride of Yeshua, not just knowing the acts of God—salvation, healing, and prosperity—like the children of Israel who were delivered from Egypt (carnal world), then murmured and complained because of the trials of the desert, mentioned in Psalm 103:7. The bride knows the ways of God through intimacy and relationship. She walks in His perfect will in order to reach the spiritual promised land, as in Hebrews 3:14-19; 4:1-3.

The Scriptures tell us the foolish virgins will be cast into "outer darkness." The Greek word *Skotos* means "outer darkness," and comes from the root word *Skia*, which means "shade or shadow." It is not pitch black in reference to Hell, but a lack of light—such as being outside of the Glory of God. If compared to the light from the Glory of God in the

Holy of Holies in the Tabernacle, the outer court could be described as shady. The bride will dwell in the Holy of Holies, while the foolish virgins will not be allowed to enter in.

The Bride is Spiritually Mature

And the damsel *was* very fair to look upon, a
virgin, neither had any man known her.

—Genesis 24:16

In Genesis 24, we see Eliezer coming for Rebekah, a
damsel and a virgin—just as Yeshua is going to come for a
spiritually mature bride, not a baby Christian who has not
reached spiritual adulthood and isn't old enough to marry.

The Hebrew word for "damsel" is *Na'arah*, which
means "a girl from infancy to adolescence." This is a
prophetic picture of the Bride of Christ who has grown to
spiritual maturity. She is old enough to marry.

A spiritual child is a carnal Christian (saved, but
babes in Christ). They are carnally minded, controlled by the
flesh, and not able to learn and understand the deeper truths
of God's Word. They live on simple truth, "as newborn
babes."

We see in 1 Corinthians 3:1-2:

And I, brethren, could not speak unto you as unto spiritual, but as unto carnal, *even* as unto babes in Christ. I have fed you with milk, and not with meat: for hitherto ye were not able *to bear* it, neither yet now are you able.

The Scriptures tell us in 1 Peter 3:18 that we are to grow in grace—like the parable of the seed, we are to mature in the understanding of God and kingdom principles. We are to leave the elementary things and grow into spiritual maturity. For Hebrews 6:1 says: "Therefore, leaving the principles of the doctrine of Christ, let us go on to perfection."

The Greek word for "perfection" is *Teliotace*, which means "completeness and full maturity." The root word *Telios* means "completeness, full grown, adult, and mature."

Our goal as believers is not just salvation. We are to strive for perfection and grow in knowledge, having a deeper understanding of God's ways, entering into a deeper intimacy with Him. By growing from faith to faith as Romans 1:17 says, by being drawn from the breast, weaned from the milk—for it is precept upon precept, line upon line, as it says in Isaiah 28:9-10.

The Bride is Given Gifts

And the servant brought forth jewels of silver,
and jewels of gold, and raiment, and gave *them*
to Rebekah.

—Genesis 24:53a

An ancient custom of Israel required the groom give
a *Mattan* ("gift" in Hebrew) to his bride at the betrothal.
This differs from the *Mohar*, which is the groom's bridal
payment to the bride's father and is an obligation of the law.

These voluntary gifts are an expression of his love
for his bride and vary greatly depending on the prosperity of
the groom. Biblical examples of this practice, such as Eliezer
giving articles of silver, gold, and garments to Rebekah, and
Shechem offering any *Mattan* for Dinah, offers its official
recognition in the marriage ceremony today.

Genesis 24:22 says, "And it came to pass, as the camels had done drinking, that the man took a golden earring of
half a shekel weight, and two bracelets for her hands of ten
shekels weight of gold."

Our bridegroom Yeshua also offers *Mattan* to His bride. Some of the gifts He gives us are eternal life and peace. And, just as Shechem did, Yeshua offers anything we ask in His name. Of course, these gifts are given to us so that we may make ourselves ready for His return.

In Matthew 7:11 we read, "If ye then, being evil, know how to give good gifts unto your children, how much more shall your Father which is in heaven give good things to them that ask him?"

Other gifts the *Ruach HaKodesh* (God's servant, the Holy Spirit) has given to Yeshua's bride are listed in 1 Corinthians 12:1, 8-10:

> Now concerning spiritual *gifts,* brethren, I would not have you ignorant... For to one is given by the Spirit the word of wisdom; to another the word of knowledge by the same Spirit; to another faith by the same Spirit; to another the gifts of healing by the same Spirit; to another the working of miracles; to another prophecy; to another discerning of spirits; to another *divers* kinds of tongues; to another the interpretation of tongues.

The Bride is a Queen

And I asked her, and said, Whose daughter *art*
thou? And she said, The daughter of Bethuel,
Nahor's son, whom Milcah bore unto him.

—Genesis 24:47

We read in the story of Isaac and Rebekah's betrothal that the wife of Abraham's brother Nahor was
Milcah. The Hebrew name *Milcah* comes from two Hebrew
words—*Malkah*, meaning "queen," and *Melech*, meaning
"king." The Hebrew name *Bethuel* is made up of *Bathah*—
meaning "desolate, waste"—and *El*—meaning God; thus
Bethuel's name means "desolate, waste of God."

Here we see that the bride is the queen of God and
comes from the out of the desolate (waste), which is symbolic of Babylon. Isaiah 62:1-5 says:

For Zion's sake will I not hold my peace,
and for Jerusalem's sake I will not rest, until the
righteousness thereof go forth as brightness,
and the salvation thereof as a lamp *that* burneth.
And the Gentiles shall see thy righteousness,
and all kings thy glory: and thou shalt be called

by a new name, which the mouth of the LORD shall name. Thou shalt also be a crown of glory in the hand of the LORD and a royal diadem in the hand of thy God. Thou shalt no more be termed Forsaken; neither shall thy land any more be termed Desolate: but thou shalt be called Hephzibah, and thy land Beulah: for the LORD delighteth in thee, and thy land shall be married. For *as* a young man marrieth a virgin, *so* shall thy sons marry thee: and *as* the bridegroom rejoiceth over the bride, *so* shall thy God rejoice over thee.

Interestingly, the Hebrew word *Beulah* means "to marry, be lord over, and husband."

The Messiah will be crowned King and His bride will be Queen, and together will rule and reign in the New Jerusalem for 1,000 years. During His Millennium reign, everyone will sojourn to the Holy City each year to celebrate the Feast of Tabernacles (Leviticus 23:41; Zechariah14:16).

In Jewish weddings, the bridegroom and bride are regarded as king and queen, dressing in elaborate clothing and wearing crowns upon their heads, while seated upon throne-like chairs, which are lifted up in jubilant revelry. This is a prophetic picture of Yeshua and His bride during the Millennium reign.

Yeshua will be crowned King and His bride will be Queen, ruling and reigning in Jerusalem for 1,000 years.

Yeshua's floral crown (crown of thorns) is replaced with many crowns. For it tells us in Revelation 19:12: "His eyes were as a flame of fire, and on his head were many crowns."

The Bride of Christ is blessed and rewarded with being a part of the first resurrection and will rule and reign with Yeshua. Revelation 20:4 describes the bride:

> And I saw thrones, and they sat upon them, and judgment was given unto them: and I saw the souls of them that were beheaded for the witness of Jesus, and for the word of God, and which had not worshiped the beast, neither his image, neither had received his mark upon their foreheads, or in their hands; and they lived and reigned with Christ for a thousand years.

Revelation 20:6 says, "Blessed and holy is he that hath part in the first resurrection: on such the second death hath no power, but they shall be priests of God and of Christ, and shall reign with him a thousand years."

The Bride is Clothed in Splendor

I will greatly rejoice in the LORD, my soul shall
be joyful in my God; for he hath clothed me
with the garments of salvation, he hath covered
me with the robe of righteousness, as a bridegroom decketh *himself* with ornaments, and as a
bride adorneth *herself* with her jewels.

—Isaiah 61:10

It was customary in ancient Israel for the host of the
marriage ceremony to provide their wedding guests with
suitable apparel. By not wearing the garments provided by
the groom's father, the guests showed a lack of appreciation
and respect for him.

In the parable of the guest improperly attired in Matthew 22:11-14, Yeshua described the king's furious reaction
to the guest who insulted him by not wearing the wedding
garments. Guests who attempt to attend the Messiah's
wedding in apparel of their own will be cast out into outer
darkness, where there is weeping and gnashing of teeth.

Matthew 22:11-14 says:

And when the king came in to see the guests, he saw there a man which had not on a wedding garment: and he saith unto him, Friend, how camest thou in hither not having a wedding garment? And he was speechless. Then said the king to the servants, Bind him hand and foot, and take him away, and cast *him* into outer darkness; there shall be weeping and gnashing of teeth. For many are called, but few *are* chosen.

As His bride, we must not seek apparel of our own choosing, such as trying to obtain salvation based upon our own good works or without true faith or repentance. In book of Esther, we see how she allowed the king's servant to choose the apparel—she did not choose her own as the others had done. We must be willing to clothe ourselves with Christ by putting on the "new man" and adorning ourselves with righteous deeds. By being ever ready to do good works, we bring glory to God. Are you doing all you can to be clothed in splendor?

Revelation 19:6-8 says:

And I heard as it were the voice of a great multitude, and as the voice of many waters, and as the voice of mighty thunderings, sayings, Alleluia: for the Lord God omnipotent reigneth. Let us be glad and rejoice, and give honor to him: for the marriage of the Lamb is come, and his wife hath made herself ready. And to her it was granted that she should be arrayed in fine linen, clean and white: for the fine linen is the righteousness of saints.

Psalm 45 is an arrangement of "The Wedding Song of the Messiah," which describes the much-anticipated marriage to the Lamb of God. Following ancient Middle Eastern tradition, the central focus rightly belongs to the bridegroom—not the bride, as is custom today. A vivid picture is given of the Bridegroom's majestic ride as He returns to meet His glorious bride! Here we see how the bride is adorned.

Psalm 45:9-15 shows us:

Kings' daughters *were* among thy honorable women: upon thy right hand did stand the queen in gold of Ophir. Hearken, O daughter, and consider, and incline thine ear; forget also thine own people, and thy father's house; so shall the king greatly desire thy beauty: for he *is* thy Lord; and worship thou him. And the daughter of Tyre *shall be there* with a gift; *even* the rich among the people shall entreat thy favor. The king's daughter *is* all glorious within: her clothing *is* of wrought gold. She shall be brought unto the king in raiment of needle-work: the virgins her companions that follow her shall be brought unto thee. With gladness and rejoicing shall they be brought: they shall enter into the king's palace.

The Bride is a Priest

Husbands, love your wives, even as Christ also
loved the church, and gave himself for it; that
he might sanctify and cleanse it with the washing of water by the word, that he might present
it to himself a glorious church, not having spot,
or wrinkle, or any such thing; but that it should
be holy and without blemish.

—Ephesians 5:25-27

Just as the high priest went before Yahweh in the
Holy of Holies on Yom Kippur (Leviticus 16), preparing
himself by "putting on" holy garments, so the Bride of
Christ must put on holy garments.

"Without spot" and "blemish" are priestly terms.
The Lord's bride will be a perfect bride, with no spot or
blemish. We are to clothe ourselves with mercy, kindness,
humility, meekness, longsuffering, forgiveness, good works,
teaching and encouraging one another.

Colossians 3:12-16 tells us:

Put on therefore, as the elect of God, holy and beloved, bowels of mercies, kindness, humbleness of mind, meekness, longsuffering; forbearing one another, and forgiving one another, if any man have a quarrel against any: even as Christ forgave you, so also *do* ye. And above all these things *put on* charity, which is the bond of perfectness. And let the peace of God rule in your hearts, to the which also ye are called in one body; and be ye thankful. Let the word of Christ dwell in you richly in all wisdom; teaching and admonishing one another in psalms and hymns and spiritual songs, singing with grace in your hearts to the Lord.

Upon approaching the well, Eliezer believed he found the right one in Rebekah, but needed to see if she met all of his expectations. With kindness and generosity she responded, which demonstrated her heart. Freely giving of herself, she served a total stranger and his animals with no expectation of anything in return.

The Bride of Christ will also be found working and serving as Rebekah was in Genesis 24:15-16. Genesis 24:17-18 shows us:

And the servant ran to meet her, and said, Let me, I pray thee, drink a little water of thy pitcher. And she said, Drink, my lord: and she hasted, and let down her pitcher upon her hand, and gave him drink.

The bride will be quick to respond to the *Ruach's* (Spirit's) voice, and will go beyond the basic requirements of service. She will have an evident willingness and desire to be joined to her Heavenly Bridegroom.

During Old Testament times, priests were instructed to teach the *Torah* of God (instruction of the law) to His people—and because all believers are called "priests of God" in the New Testament, God desires all believers to be priests before Him. Those who reject God's law (instruction, or *Torah*) will not be priests unto Him and therefore, not be His bride. Knowledge is truth and the Word of God is truth and God's instructions are truth.

Hosea 4:6 tells us:

My people are destroyed for lack of knowledge: because thou hast rejected knowledge, I will also reject thee, that thou shalt be no priest to me: seeing thou hast forgotten the law of thy God, I will also forget thy children.

> And the third day there was a marriage in Cana of Galilee; and the mother of Jesus was there: and both Jesus was called, and his disciples, to the marriage. And when they wanted wine, the mother of Jesus saith unto him, They have no wine. Jesus saith unto her, Woman, what have I to do with thee? mine hour is not yet come.
>
> —John 2:1-4

Yeshua's first miracle was at a wedding—showing the reason for His visitation to earth.

Most commentators explain this verse to mean His hour of ministry was not yet. Mary, His mother, was pushing for Him to do something, a miracle of some sort. However, this had nothing to do with the start of His earthly ministry performing a miracle. Yeshua was already a Rabbi and His ministry had already begun as He had a few of His disciples with Him. She did not ask Yeshua to do any-thing—it was He in fact, that brought this situation to the forefront. "They wanted wine"—His response to her was, "What does this have to do with me?" The governor of the feast handled the matters, such as running out of food and wine, or took it up with the bridegroom or the bridegroom's father as we see in Scripture.

Continuing in John 2:9-10, we see:

> When the ruler of the feast had tasted the water that was made wine, and knew not whence it was: (but the servants which drew the water knew;) the governor of the feast called the bridegroom, and saith unto him, Every man at the beginning doth set forth good wine; and when men have well drunk, then that which is worse: *but* thou hast kept the good wine until now.

Yeshua asked for "more wine," and His mother's response was there is no more wine. She didn't ask Him to fix the problem—this was a situation for the bridegroom, not Him. His answer insinuated, "I am not the bridegroom yet."

In Mark 2:18-20, Yeshua referred to Himself as the bridegroom:

> And the disciples of John and of the Pharisees used to fast: and they come and say unto him, Why do the disciples of John and of the Pharisees fast, but thy disciples fast not? And Jesus said unto them, Can the children of the bridechamber fast, while the bridegroom is with them? as long as they have the bridegroom

with them, they cannot fast. But the days will come, when the bridegroom shall be taken away from them, and then shall they fast in those days.

John the Baptist also referred to Yeshua as the bridegroom in John 3:28-30:

Ye yourselves bear me witness, that I said, I am not the Christ, but that I am sent before him. He that hath the bride is the bridegroom: but the friend of the bridegroom, which standeth and heareth him, rejoiceth greatly because of the bridegroom's voice: this my joy therefore is fulfilled. He must increase, but I *must* decrease.

In Yeshua's first recorded miracle at the wedding at Cana, He shows us when His hour "as the bridegroom" will be and that this is a prophetic charade of His true reason for coming to the earth.

The six stone pots are six days of creation, which is 6,000 years (2 Peter 3:8). These stone pots were 20-30 gallon earthen vessels, used for ceremonial washing—thus, unclean. They were filled to brim with new wine—symbolizing the abundance and overflowing joy we can have with Him. This wine also represents the Sabbath, or seventh day—the 1,000-year rest for the earth when He reigns.

Stone water pots, once used in the Jewish custom of washing outward parts, were now filled to the brim with new wine, symbolic of the inward cleansing power and new life we have with Yeshua!

Delight must have filled the young groom's heart as he tasted it, knowing the Savior blessed his marriage with an overflowing abundance of wine. Now the week-long celebration could continue, with the *Sheva B'rachot* blessings spoken over the second cup of wine, sealing the marriage covenant. For a wedding is incomplete without this. This is why Yeshua said in Matthew 26:29: "I will not drink henceforth of this fruit of the vine, until that day when I drink it new with you in my Father's kingdom."

The bride is now betrothed to her Heavenly Bridegroom, and our marriage to Yeshua will not be complete until we are in Heaven and share this second cup of wine with Him, just as He said in Matthew 26:29. He has saved the very best for last! We must be faithful until that day!

The Bride has a New Home

Awake, awake; put on thy strength, O Zion; put on thy beautiful garments, O Jerusalem, the holy city: for henceforth there shall no more come into thee the uncircumcised and the unclean.

—Isaiah 52:1

After the Millennium reign (seventh day), the new heaven and new earth will appear. It is the eighth day, time for a new beginning. The number "eight" in the Scriptures refers to "new beginnings."

Revelation tells us in 20:10-15 that the earth is finally cleansed from all sin and unrighteousness. Judgment takes place and Satan has been cast into the lake of fire and brimstone. Now, in Revelation 21 we see the new heaven and new earth. There is no mention of the Bride of Christ until Revelation 21, when we see her coming down out of Heaven.

At the end of the 1,000 years, the Messiah will present His bride, holy and spotless to Himself. This is to fulfill her week of purification according to the law of Moses

(Leviticus 12:2-4; Luke 2:22). Women in the Bible are a picture of the church, or bride, but this uncleanness also applied to men having the eighth day set apart for circumcision—a day of dedication. Scriptures tells us that Mary was unable to enter the Temple until the eighth day with Yeshua, because both she and Joseph were unclean. We see in Leviticus 15:28-29:

> But if she be cleansed of her issue, then she shall number to herself seven days, and after that she shall be clean. And on the eighth day she shall take unto her two turtles, or two young pigeons, and bring them unto the priest, to the door of the tabernacle of the congregation.

The church will not enter into God's holy temple (New Jerusalem) until the eighth day—until all the sin of the earth is removed. Our hearts are made clean by the repentance and forgiveness of sins, but everyday we are in contact with unclean things—television, radio, magazines—and are still defiled. The earth will be cleansed and made new on the eighth day.

Mary, a picture of the bride, is unclean (defiled by the earth) until the eighth day.

In Luke 2:22-24 we read:

And when the days of her purification according to the law of Moses were accomplished, they brought him to Jerusalem, to present him to the Lord; (as it is written in the law of the Lord, Every male that openeth the womb shall be called holy to the Lord;) and to offer a sacrifice according to that which is said in the law of the Lord, A pair of turtledoves, or two young pigeons.

In the book of Revelation, the bride is revealed in chapter 21:2, after the new heaven and new earth are created: "And I John saw the holy city, new Jerusalem, coming down from God out of heaven, prepared as a bride adorned for her husband."

The Hebrew word for "virgin," *B'toolah*, also refers to "city and state," and here it is interchangeable:

The Scriptures tell us nothing unclean or defiled shall enter in—only those that have made themselves ready. That is the Bride of Christ.

We see in Revelation 21:27, "And there shall in no wise enter into it any thing that defileth, neither whatsoever worketh abomination, or maketh a lie: but they which are written in the Lamb's book of life."

The New Jerusalem coming down from heaven is the beautiful place that Yeshua has been preparing for us.

And we see the bride is now referred to as the Lamb's wife—the marriage has now been consummated.

Revelation 21:9 reads, "And there came unto me one of the seven angels which had the seven vials full of the seven last plagues, and talked with me, saying, Come hither, I will show thee the bride, the Lamb's wife."

And I have set thee *so*: thou wast upon the holy
mountain of God.

—Ezekiel 28:14b

The angel is showing John (who is the bride) the
New Jerusalem from a great and high mountain.

In Revelation 21:10 we find, "And he carried me
away in the spirit to a great and high mountain, and showed
me that great city, the holy Jerusalem, descending out of
heaven from God."

In Scriptures, we see how the bride is on the Holy
Mountain of God (Mount Zion now), instead of Lucifer.
Satan no longer has access on the Holy Mountain of God
because he exalted himself and his own beauty. He used his
God-given wisdom for selfish gain. It is interesting to note
that Lucifer was described as having some of the same
characteristics as the Bride of Christ. John describes the
bride in Revelation 21:11, "Having the glory of God: and her
light *was* like unto a stone most precious, even like a jasper
stone, clear as crystal."

The bride will be ordained with all manner of precious stones—how Lucifer is also described in Ezekiel 28.

Ezekiel 28:13 says:

> Thou hast been in Eden the garden of God; every precious stone *was* thy covering, the sardius, topaz, and the diamond, the beryl, the onyx, and the jasper, the sapphire, the emerald, and the carbuncle, and gold: the workmanship of thy tabrets and of thy pipes was prepared in thee in the day that thou wast created.

Lucifer was created to give praise and worship to God. Most believers are familiar with Satan as the worship leader of Heaven. This is probably true, but Scriptures also describe Him as a picture of what we shall be.

Jeremiah 31:4 tells us, "Again I will build thee, and thou shalt be built, O virgin of Israel: thou shalt again be adorned with thy tabrets, and shalt go forth in the dances of them that make merry."

In the last days, we will again learn to use this instrument, the *tabret*, and Satan hates it because it is a spiritual weapon against him—a reminder of what he lost. He is the "other woman" and hates the church, Yeshua's bride.

Ezekiel 28:15 reads, "Thou *wast* perfect in thy ways from the day thou wast created, till iniquity was found in thee."

Lucifer was perfect in all his ways until iniquity was found in him—just as Yeshua's bride will be perfect and without blemish.

The Hebrew word for "perfect" is *Tamim*. This is the same word in Exodus 12:5 that describes the Passover Lamb—without blemish. Before Lucifer fell, he was without blemish. This is also the same word used in Psalm 119:1, translated as "undefiled." God is telling us that those who are spiritually mature before God walk in the law of God.

Just as Satan was thrown out of God's presence because iniquity was found in him, the bride cannot enter into God's presence with iniquity in her heart. We cannot serve our own purposes and serve God.

Are you prepared to enter His presence? Have you made yourself ready for the royal wedding to the Lamb of God? The Lord desires a bride suited for Him.

Conclusion

In this book, we have studied the following characteristics that must be found in the Bride of Christ:

1. The bride is a damsel and a virgin.
2. The bride is known for her righteous acts and deeds.
3. The bride is a church—holy, cleansed, and washed by the Word of God.
4. The bride is a priest, perfect without spot or wrinkle.
5. The bride is a remnant and comes out from the body of Messiah.
6. The bride is sincerely devoted to Yeshua.
7. The bride is a watchful intercessor.

About Rebecca at the Well

Rebecca at the Well Foundation is a non-profit Judeo-Christian organization devoted to inspiring believers to prepare for the return of the Messiah. By informing the "called out ones" the way to walk in the beauty of holiness, it motivates members of the body to be clothed with righteous acts and deeds as the Bride of Messiah.

In an effort to bridge the gap between Judaism and Christianity, Rebecca at The Well Foundation provides workshops and seminars about the Hebraic roots of our faith that binds us together as one. All believers can celebrate Yeshua's return as they learn how to make themselves ready as a pure and holy bride.

Rebecca Park Totilo, founder and president of the Rebecca at The Well Foundation, is currently touring the country, preparing the bride for her Heavenly Bridegroom. She is available to speak at conferences, seminars and retreats. Please contact her at (727) 688-2115 for more information, or if you would like to have her come and share with your group or congregation.

Visit our website at:
www.rebeccaatthewell.org or www.ratw.org

For e-mail correspondence:
becca@RebeccaAtTheWell.org

For snail mail correspondence:
Rebecca At The Well Foundation
PO Box 60044
St. Petersburg, FL 33784

Lightning Source UK Ltd.
Milton Keynes UK
UKOW031952140412

190762UK00006B/5/P